Amber's Wings

**Sun shining
Birds singing
Wind blowing
Hearts beating
Eyes closing
Angels flying**

Written and Illustrated by
Debbie Simms and Donna Simms

Copyright 2015 by Debbie Simms & Donna Simms

Published by Wood Islands Prints/Tom Schultz; 670 TCH, RR1; Belle River, PE, C0A 1B0; Canada; schultz@pei.sympatico.ca; www.woodislandsprints.com

Debbie Simms studied art & Graphic Design. She enjoys painting, gardening and going to the beach, spending time with her family & friends, especially her great nephew Kaiden and great nieces Phinley and Zoey. A special thank-you to her past fellow co-workers, (Basket Kase) Shirley, Mae, Marion, Christine, and Darla.

Donna Simms studied colour theory & Graphic Design, She enjoys going to the movies, landscaping, going to the beach, spending time with great nephew Kaiden and great nieces Phinley and Zoey, and family & friends. Thank-you to her fellow Staples co-workers, past and present.

AMBER

This story was inspired to give comfort to children (and adults) when dealing with a loss of a pet.

Dedicated to the memory
of our cherished Aunt, Sheila Osler.
On a warm day in May, with the gentle wind bringing the aroma of freshly cut roses and sea salt air, you are walking along the Cape Cod shore with your furry friends, Digger, Lady, Peanut and Prince. Your Soul Is Now Free!

On that cool
crisp December morning
all the houses were decorated with
red satin bows and glowing lights.
This was going to be an extra special
Christmas. The day was finally here.
I was getting a puppy!

As I glanced into a wooden pen filled with rambunctious puppies, I had eyes only for a tiny female puppy, with white markings down her face, a black button nose, a speckled belly, snow-white paws, and white on the tip of her tail. As I cuddled the tiny fluffy cedar-smelling ball of fur in my arms, I knew in my heart that she was the one.

When we arrived home, I carried the squirmy puppy up the stairs to the kitchen. She stumbled around, not knowing what to make of it all. She sniffed around from room to room. Then she found a spot that seemed safe. She squeezed her body into the end of the coffee table!

We named her Misty, but that just didn't suit her. It sounded more like a cat's name. Her fur colour changed from a golden butterscotch to a shiny brilliant ginger colour, so she became 'Amber'. When she got into mischief, she was 'Amber Janie'. Her favourite toy was a chewed-up red rubber ball.

Amber got into a lot of mischief. She played with anything in sight; old smelly socks, torn slippers and holey mittens. She would toss my fluffy pink earmuffs in the air.

Amber would unroll rolls of toilet paper,
and chew and shred newspapers.

As a puppy, Amber was timid. She grew from a small stocky puppy into a grown dog, but she was still a puppy at heart. She would greet you with a sharp, loud bark and a wagging tail, pounce on you, and lick your face.

Amber enjoyed being outside in nature, surrounded with chirping birds, fluttering butterflies, and buzzing bees.

Amber loved to dig holes. With her face covered in dirt, she would poke her head up and look very mischievous. She would also lie in the cool soil, and would hide her old chewed up bones in a pile of dirt. Then she would leave dirty paw prints on the newly washed floors.

The warmth of a summer day prompted a drive to the beach. With the car windows open, Amber popped her head out to smell the salt sea air. As we walked along the beach, the water sparkled and glistened. She left paw prints in the warm sand, but as the rippling tide came ashore, they were washed away

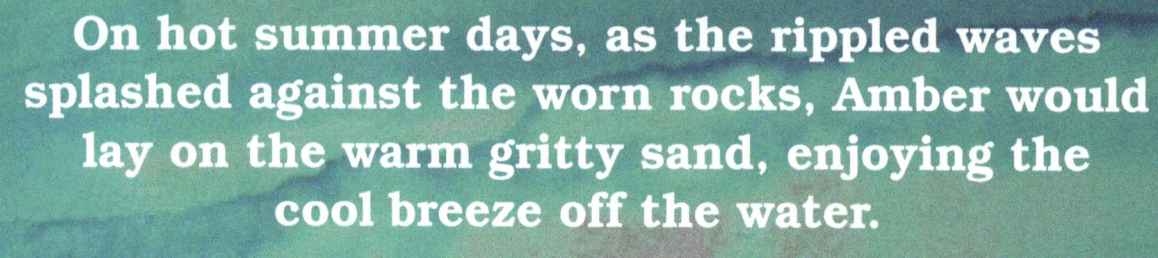

On hot summer days, as the rippled waves splashed against the worn rocks, Amber would lay on the warm gritty sand, enjoying the cool breeze off the water.

Years later, when I looked into Amber's big weary eyes, I still saw the eight-week-old, playful puppy that filled our lives and hearts with so much love. Amber was walking slower, and her face and whiskers were a bit whiter, but she still had a zest for life.

Twinkling glowing stars filled the evening sky.
Amber was snuggled tightly in my arms,
with the wind blowing gently
and we looked way up to the sky.
With tears in my eyes, I told her that
one day she would go to Heaven,
and asked her to show me a sign so
I would know she was watching over me.
I never wanted to let her go,
but in my heart I knew one day
she would pass away.

Fluffy white marshmallow clouds filled the blue sky. A bright orange glow surrounded the early morning sun that shone brightly through the lush green fir trees.

As the vet carried Amber outside, she looked so peaceful. A golden light surrounded her. I gently placed Amber on a fluffy blanket underneath a fir tree. A flood of memories flashed through my head. I held her in my arms, as I did so many times before, but this would be the last time.

Minutes later Amber passed away surrounded by love at the age of sixteen.

Looking at the clouds is a wondrous and magical experience. Way, way up in the bright blue sky the floating fluffy white clouds form shapes.

In that moment, your imagination is free to discover things in the clouds: a puppy, a cat, or a horse. To us these are gifts from Amber and her fairy angels... fairies that protect and guide our pets to Heaven.

While sitting outside, enjoying the warmth of the sun, my thoughts were on Amber, thinking about all the wonderful memories. One patch of blue sky had the shape of Amber.

Another time, after planting flowers in memory of a sweet Airedale dog named Annie, I looked up at the sky, and there in the clouds was the shape of a dog... Annie.

While out for a brisk walk on a cool
autumn day, I again glanced up to see clouds
formed in the shape of Amber, lying with her head
resting on her favourite speckled milk bone pillow.

One cool winter day, with snowflakes fluttering around, I dressed in my warm plaid coat to play outside. Lying in the snow making a snow angel, I glanced up at the bright blue sky. There were fluffy clouds forming the shape of Amber's face.

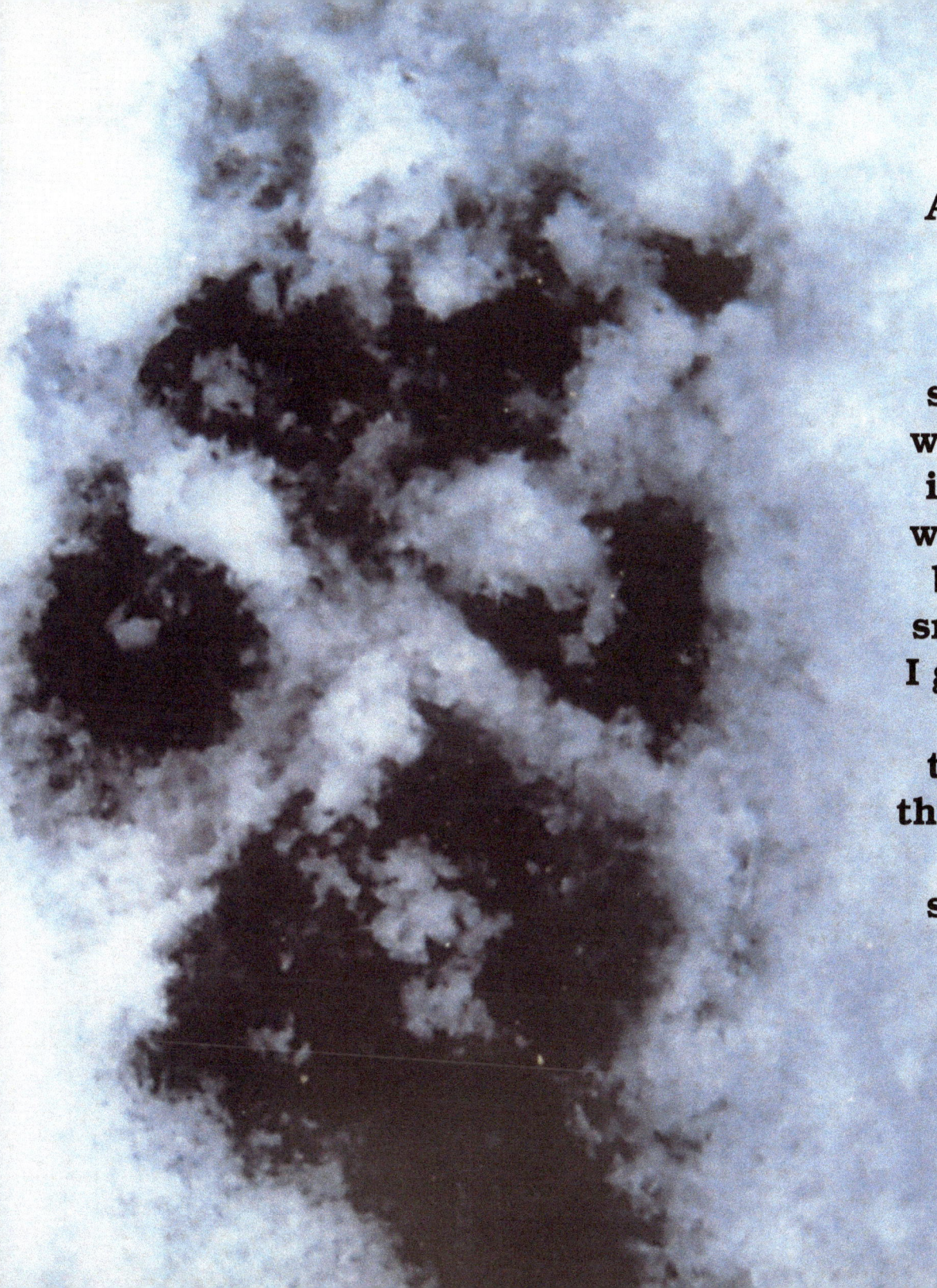

Another time, after a winter storm, I went out into the whirling, blowing snow. As I glanced down, there in the fallen snow I saw one huge single paw print.

On an early Sunday drive, while gazing at the fluffy clouds slowly moving through the sky, a cloud suddenly started to form the shape of a medieval horse.

Since Amber passed away, I see fluttering butterflies every day. Little dainty white and apricot coloured butterflies flutter around in a swirling motion. It looks magical as though they are sprinkling fairy dust.

Once as I rested my head on a soft fluffy pillow, my mind drifted off to a magical place called Heaven. My guardian Angel, a sweet little girl named Angela took my hand. She was wearing a beautiful white gown with satin bows and had golden coloured hair. She took my hand and said, "No, you want to open *this* door." Wide eyed, with the door ajar, I was amazed at what I saw.

There was a room filled with lots of children and adults. I glanced through the crowds until my eyes focused on someone I knew and loved, my cherished Grandma Kaye. I ran into her arms. I told her I missed her so much, and Amber too.

Grandma said, "I know you do Sweetie." She told me to look outside at the beautiful green pasture with rolling hills surrounded by lush evergreens. There were dogs running and playing.

"Grandma, I don't see Amber."

"Look closer."

With tears rolling down my face I asked, "Is that Amber?"

"Yes dear !

"But Grandma, her fur colour looks different, like a brilliant glowing orange sun."

Grandma said that is because the sun shines so brightly in heaven. She promised to cuddle Amber, and look after her until I come to heaven.

Pets That Have Left Paw Prints In Our Hearts Forever

(Dog), Amber, Skippy, Beauty, Molly, Sandy, Maggie, Sadie, Buffy, Nipper, Teddy, Smudge, Digger, Lady, Prince, Peanut, Hula, Snickers, Jazz, Floyd, Bowie, Emma, Ella, Jed, Coltrane, Clancy, Buster, Britta, Tiki, Caymus, Freddy, Lily, Sophie, Sheba, Mattie, Annie, Copper, Penny, Ben, Scoutt, Trail, Jib, Achilles, Shelby, Little Johnny, Argus, Buster, Demon, Manitou, Kimber, Chevy, Hersey, Sasha, Sally, Dion, Abby, Sparky, Aleea, Shema, Jasmine, Rose, Jet, Piper, Boomerang, Samantha, Toby, Alfred, Dude, Scampie, Max, Ellie, Toto, Myra, Riley, Buddy, Sampson, Tiny, Pepper, Spirit, Chole, Hagen, P2, Que, Willie, Kelsey, Nella, Hobbes, Bailey, Benji, Jenny, Tsugi, Radar, Quincy, Henry, Duke, Casey, Rascal, Peppermint, Lizzie, Nala, Doban, Connor, Ceilidh, Coda, Shanon, Gracie, Marshall, Shadow, Pongo, Belle, Cleo, Gizzie, Tuc, Tanner, Ty, Baby Bear, Theo, Niki, Lucas, Sneekers, Cosmo, Chubby, Charlie, Kaboom, Tipie, Schooner, Becky, Schenley, Daisy, Odie, Darby

(Cat), Sammy, Meeko, Sassy, Carl, Zeus, Jessie, Ollie, Guinness, Snowball, Princess, Muffin's, Shundy, Nella, Maggie, Azrael, Lizzie, Snoopy, Woodstock, Wally, Sugar, Normy, Misty, Tinker, Julia, Silken, Fritz, Amber, Peppermint, Fluffy, Mittens, Meisha, Shema, Kitty, Buddy, Charlie, Callie, Merp, Niki, Coco, Azrad, Mitz, Mr. Nooners, Jean-Pierre Mccoy, Murray, Pretty Boy, Tabitha, Fantasia, Blackie

(Bunny) Dustbuster

(Bird) Beaker

(Horse) Rene, Sergeant Pepper

(Pony) Hobbes, Dapple Dee, Honeysu

In Memory Of Amber (May Your Star Shine Bright)

(A fond memory is Great Nephew Kaiden waving to Amber)

A heartfelt thank-you to: Dr. Paul Donovan, Dr. Sue Cochrane, Dr. Andrea Studzinski, Dr. Oriana Raab, Dr. Hans Gelens, Paula Forrest-Mackinnon, & Veterinary Class Of (2013), (Atlantic Veterinary College); Kelleigh Waters, Ariana Verrilli, Frannie Allan, Sophie Whoriskey, Zoe Launcelott, Caitlin Leclair, Lisa Connor, Lucy Cohen, Lisa Gillis, Kyle Vititoe, Shari Reheb, Jennifer Hurford, Sonja Sandhu, Nikky Macleod, Nichelle Peck, Danielle Collins, Samantha Marquis, Susan Taylor.

A special thank-you to Karen Forrest
Your Soul Is Now Free

In Loving Memory: Loving Grandparents Kaye & Charles Skinner & Ida & Douglas Simms, (Aunt) Sheila Osler, (Aunt) Jessie Simms, (Uncle) Bobby Simms, Friends: Kathy Bushell, Bob Mackey, James Jearvis.

In memory of a dear friend: Joan Rice (Joan's oil paints & watercolours were used in this book.) She is walking along the beach with her beloved dogs Ben & Scoutt.

Thanks So Much for all Your support: Kathy & Sterling Simms (Parents), (Nephew) Kyle & (Jodi) Blackman, Madison Kelly, (Niece) Katelynn Blackman, (Aunt) Donna Macleod, (Uncle) Ross Osler, Dave & Lillian Younker, Kathy Jearvis, Friends: Margaret & Adam & Mary Kiprenko, Janice Donaldson, Kerry MacMillan, June Large, Doreen Mackey, Jenny & David Gallant, Lori-Ann & Paul Mansbridge, Nancy & Bill Zahavich, Jessica Rock, Lindsay Strout, and Rosette Parker, Don & Dorothy Reynolds.

Painting by Sterling Simms

Since a few people... according to the authors, only four out of a hundred... cannot identify the patterns in the clouds, here are 'keys' to the cloud pictures presented in this book.

www.ingramcontent.com/pod-product-compliance
Lightning Source LLC
Chambersburg PA
CBHW040005080526
44586CB00027B/2891